THE BHYABACHYAKA
AND OTHER WILD POEMS

The Bhyabachyaka and other Wild Poems

Sampurna Chattarji Eurig Salisbury

Illustrated by

Saswata and Susruta Mukherjee

SCHOLASTIC
New York Toronto London Auckland
Sydney New Delhi Hong Kong

Published by Scholastic India Pvt. Ltd.
A subsidiary of Scholastic Inc., New York, 10012 (USA).
Publishers since 1920, with international operations in Canada, Australia, New Zealand, the United Kingdom, India, and Hong Kong.

First edition: November 2019

ISBN-13: 978-93-8929-771-3

Printed in India at EIH Limited - Unit Printing Press,
IMT Manesar, Gurugram (Haryana).

A MESSAGE FROM SCHOLASTIC INDIA

Hello there young reader!

So, the cover caught your eye, eh? You know, I thought the longest word that existed was 'supercalifragilisticexpialidocious'. Until this book came along and I learnt that there's an even longer word!

Don't believe me? Turn to page 90 and take a deep breath.

This book is #hundred #percent #nonsense #genius. Why wouldn't it be? It's got two of the funniest and zaniest minds at work.

Go ahead, the Bhyabachyaka is calling.

Shantanu Duttagupta
Publisher

for

Aabir
Ahvaan
Ava
Caradog
Emma
Ewen
Kaarin
Llew
Meera
Mia
Miraya
Nia
Noëllie
Tara
Veer

CONTENTS

CULTURALLY MEANINGFUL WORDS
(One Word, Two Poems)

PLACE NAMES: LONG AND SHORT

Hello and Shwmae!

Welcome to a world that celebrates the beautiful beastliness and wondrous whimsicality of words. As poets, as friends, we began our word-swap project some years ago, while conducting a poetry workshop in Bangalore (now Bengaluru).

Swapping words from Cymraeg (Welsh) and Bangla (Bengali), we took full advantage of the mischief and goofiness of words we didn't understand, words we had just learnt and words we had plucked straight out of our heads. We loved playing with words—existing and invented—to make all these poems.

We hope you will love reading them, tasting delicious new sounds and meeting all kinds of creatures, characters, emotions and experiences. Enjoy!

Sampurna and Eurig
(also known as SC and ES)

BANGLA-WELSH WORDS

I hear him when I'm writing,
The Bhyabachyaka choking,
A crow-like bird on my window sill
Choking on his food with skill.

His cry is like a hearty croak,
He stands there in his blue-black cloak,
The Bhyabachyaka, calmly choking
On the sill while I am writing.

It's not a llama from Paloma
Nor a llano in the pllano.
It's not Llorente from Firenze
Nor a llerena-singing soprano.

It's not Llareggub in a bathing tub
Nor a llanero in a sombrero.
It's not Llanelli in white flannellis
Fast-bowling with a Ferrero.

It's not the llanito-speaking pllanito
Nor a Lleida-lassoing rider.
It's not a llamoid going ovoid
Over a lleullin-spinning spider.

What it is—is a mystery
About the last men on Ly
Mentally distracted by
The Sten Mall on Y

Who chased the letter S
Up the Nelly Mast
Where a small yen for T
Brought them down really fast

Relaxing on a beach
They caught a smelly tan
And made the letter M
Yell noisily for Stan

Who fled instead to NY
To live with darling Stella
And L for Lyn (their lady dog)
In a jazzed-up steamy cellar.

'The Mishmishey,' the great man said
In a wishy-washy voice,
'Once lived upon the mountain sides,
But now lives here by choice.'

'Here at the zoo,' he said at length,
'It sees all manner of things
That otherwise it wouldn't have,
That's why it hardly sings.'

'Its natural habitat,' he said,
'Is in the upper branches, look!
We moved the trees for convenience—
For details, see my book.'

'The Mishmishey,' he said at last,
'Was once endangered in the wild,
But now the wild's in danger, well,
It's far better off inside.'

CRAIR

– SC

Will someone give me some crair?
I really need to breathe!
It's too cramped and crowded here
I'm about to seethe!

It isn't creepy to need some crair
It isn't cranky-cross—
It's simply crepuscular
Like a crescent crimp of moss.

Everyone needs some crair
Even a khargosh on a mission
To sleep his way through a race
Towards finicular fission.

When your stomach grumbles hungrily
You're in dire need of crair!
Oh, please, order some jaldiquick
Before I faint into the mair!

Joborjong could turn his hand
To any job in town
(Also, he could turn his hand
Three sixty degrees around).

Joborjong could mend a car
And fix its carburettor
(And he could also recommend
Someone who'd do it better).

Joborjong could overhaul
An old decrepit plane
(Mind you, the poor thing overall
Would never fly again).

Whatever the job, rain or shine,
Then poor old Joborjong
Could be counted on (without fail)
To be right bang in the wrong.

What fructose is to fruit
Ffrwchnedd is to feeling
What fructose is to sugar
Ffrwchnedd is to ceiling

What frugal is to famine
Ffrwchnedd is to mouth
What frugal is to budget
Ffrwchnedd is to south

What frumious is to Bandersnatch
Ffrwchnedd is to fun
What frumious is to Wonderland
Ffrwchnedd is to sun

No, my friend, you've got it wrong!
Ffrwchnedd is a fright,
The kind you get when smog and smoke
Block out all the stars at night.

You've no clue what Ffrwchnedd is!
Ffrwchnedd is a frazzle,
The kind that hits you in the gut
When you're too dull to dazzle.

Dhath! It's neither this nor that!
Let me start again:

Ffrwchnedd is a frail old soul
With water in his brain.

Ffrwchnedd is a freighter
Carrying French fries down the coast.
Ffrwchnedd is a fresco
Of Frankenstein crunching toast.

Poor Ffrwchnedd playing Frisbee—
Once so fine and free—

Is now so sadly gated
By the confusion of his name—

Frayed, frowning and frustrated,
He fried and froze his fame.

It's blessed with the loveliest bloom,
Nicer than a rose, it fills the room
With the neatest, sleekest, sweetest scent,
Its glorious essence heaven sent,
Its petals curled, by angels kissed,
Its touch akin to a mountain mist ...

Hang on, why haven't I heard of them, though?

Would you like a bunch of Gordobhs?

No.

I love your voice when it's strong, I love it when it's weak.
But best of all, I love it when it utterly can't speak

Having forgotten all the words in every language but one—
And in that language can recall just THIS word (run?)—

Clindarddach, your voice says, ragged to the core
Like an aching tongue walking miles with a footsore.

('Ugh—the very thought of a tongue trailing on roads!'
'What's wrong with that? No worse than kissing toads!')

Clindarddach, your voice says, as if risen from a grave
Coughing bits of earth and stone,
Clindarddach, your voice says, spitting bits of bone.

('How gross! Can't we talk of something else?'
'Like what? Amoebae? Self-dividing selves?')

Clindarddach, your voice says, getting back into the poem
Like an insomniac vagabond climbing into bed,
Clindarddach, your voice says, as you cover up your head.

('Ah! That's sweet! At last, some happy stuff!'
'You quite deserve it, for being such a muff!')

Ragged, footsore, forgotten, unravelled and undone
Wishing only a bit too late you hadn't had such fun.

Under a cloak of darkness, you're clinging to a vakh
Stringing out a melody that would make poor old Bach

Turn over in his ancient grave as you let out a feeble snore—
Clindarddach, your voice says, and then, alas, no more.

Sweet meat,
Once a treat,
What wouldn't I give
To eat

Its identical
Soft tentacles!
I'd give every cent
To cull

Just one again,
Yes, I would drain
The oceans all if they
Contained

A lone supply
(I think I'd cry)
Of its bespeckled wings,
And I

Would take a swipe
At the old snipe
Who slipped the last one
Down its pipe!

What shall I do with Dibyn-Dobyn?
Shall I change his name to Bobby?
Shall I change my own to Libby?
Shall I change *yours* to Simply-Sobby?

Oh!

What shall I do with Dibyn-Dobyn?
Shall I give him first dibs?
Shall I banish him forever?
Shall I shush him when he cribs?

Ah!

What shall I do with Dibyn-Dobyn?
Shall I drop him in the bin?
Shall I find him a new hobby?
Shall I give him lactogin?

Eh!

What shall I do with Dibyn-Dobyn?
Shall I smack him on the gob?
Shall I seat him in the lobby?
Shall I sack him from the job?

Ei!

What shall I do with Dibyn-Dobyn?
Shall I buy him a little bib?
Shall I treat him to tandoori?
Shall I tell him a big fat fib?

In old age it was hard to see her
For the children come to hear
From her teeming lips the story,
How she won her fame and glory.

At six years old she'd sold a song
To buy an oxcart stout and strong,
'But where's your ox?' the seller asked,
'My songs,' she said, 'pull off that task.'

'You're funny, you,' the seller laughed
And went away, but by her craft
In two days' time she had a throng
Of people pulling for a song.

Her fame increased, a Poet heard,
Who thought the notion quite absurd,
'You've got some cheek,' the Poet sung,
'Yes, two,' she said, 'they house my tongue.'

'You're shameless, you,' the Poet spat
And went to tell the others that
A girl in town of little size
Was selling songs unauthorized.

And then the elders summoned her
In grave despair to where they were,
'What's this we've heard about your squall?'
'Yes, quite,' she said, and sang her all.

'She's dangerous!' the elders brayed,
And to their eyes their great hall swayed
And creaked and cracked as if a storm
Had swelled inside as she performed.

They all rushed out and, as they did,
In came the people riveted.
'Listen, listen,' they said, 'this bird
Sings the loveliest song we've heard.'

Who else but Dant can get his teeth into a twist?
Who else but Dant can play no tricks at whist?

Who else but Dant can brush up on his sums
While polishing to pink his cutely bleeding gums?

Who else but Dant thinks halitosis is a boon
As he picks his cavities and begins to croon?

Who else but Dant
can write the *Divine Comedy*
(without a single 'e')?

Who else but Dant
can hold forth on philosophy
        (without a single 'p')?

Who else but Dant
can wear braces
meant for bears (polar)

by sizing them down
to fit
his giant molar?

Who else but Dant
can bite a dog
and get away
        with rabies?

Who else but Dant
can ply his canines
to entertain
        all the babies?

Who else but Dant
can floss while figure-skating
for better dental health
        and higher TV-rating?

Who else but Dant
can chew a twig at dawn
to keep his pearly-whites green
as a freshly-mowed lawn?

As the questions come fast and furious, tangling up the schemes, here's the one and only question that really knows what it means:

If Dant can't
then who can?

[stunned and awe-full silence]

INVENTED WORDS

CAFFALACIOUS

I get so tired out sometimes,
So, so tired of finding rhymes,
Of writing, describing,
Creating, concocting,
I throw my pencil on the ground
And make a caffalacious sound!

The Cyffrablaidd lives in Cuffe Parade in a kumra
the size of a coin.
The Cyffrablaidd got in a lufda once for stealing
gold cuff links.
The Cyffrablaidd caught a cough and a cold
And ended up in a ditch,
But being a very blithe bird
It recovered and made itself rich.

Don't worry if you can't find it, look again with a new pair of sharpened eyes at a view cropped to a fence, a clump of grass, a row of fenceposts and a tree, nothing you haven't seen before, and force yourself nicely to let the the meaning slip, almost like learning to write with your other hand, so if you can't see the bird in the branches wearing a bright blue tuxedo and big loud rainbow braces: don't worry, look again.

Sinking into
a pool of glue,
the fisherman went
Plwb!

Spinning round
a spool of yarn,
the weaverbird went
Plwb!

Slurping up
a spill of milk,
the tiger cub went
Plwb!

Swooping down
a swirl of air,
the baby boy went
Plwb!

A po
em
does
not simp
ly come f
rom nowh
ere.

It build
s up in
side you f
or some
times a d
ay, more oft
en years.

It boils
and bub
bles, congeals
and smooths
and liqui
fies aga
in.

Then,
once it's read
y, when your
in
ner ear p
ings and p
ops,

out burs
st three siz
zling
drops ...
wordy
gurdy
boom!

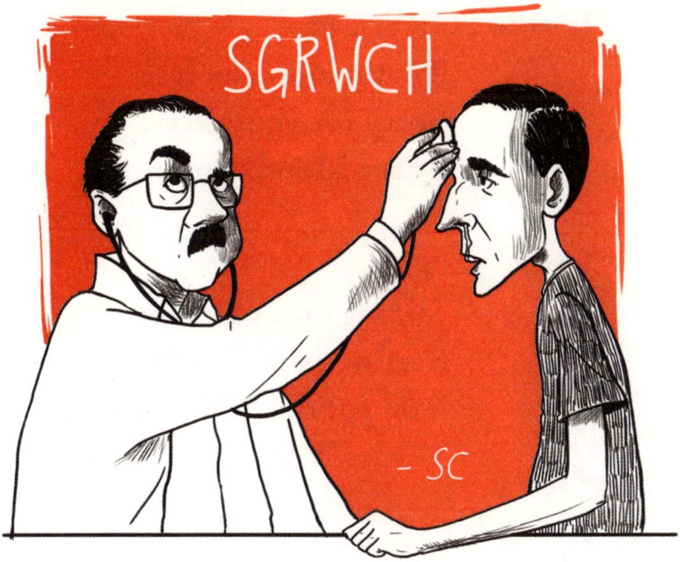

You've got a SGRWCH somewhere
Possibly in your head
Possibly in your toes
Possibly in the centre
Of your—pardon—snotty nose.

There's no point in pretending
By shaking your head
Or wiggling your toes
Even—I beg your pardon—
By picking your runny nose

That you DON'T have a SGRWCH somewhere.

Own up!

It’s the SGRWCH
That makes you feel
Sorry for yourself
Every Monday morning

Until
Sliding on a ghich-pich
Sorting every khich-pich
You put the SGRWCH
Where it belongs—

In hell.

He joined the circus at three years old,
For three small banyan seeds was sold
To a caravan of clowns, who cared
For him and loved him so—they shared
The work between them as he grew,
What things the jesters knowed he knew.

And so at six he could easily soak
With his fake flower all manner of folk,
At nine, he mimed for one full day
And never gave the ruse away,
He wrote his own gags at eighteen
And wowed the world with his routine.

But then he stopped. For inside out
He knew his trade and had no doubt,
No doubt at all about his knack
For throwing pies like a maniac.
One day he stated where he sat,
'I'd like to be an acrobat!'

His insides swayed, he wavered then,
But said the same words once again,
And all the clowns cried bucketfuls
Of tears and wailed like dying gulls,
Yet after an hour, they said, 'No, no.
We'll help you,' for they loved him so.

He learnt the ropes, the highs and lows,
And each and every time he froze
Upon a lofty line, or fell,
The clowns would shout, 'You're doing well!'
And step by step he crossed, one day,
A soaring string without a sway.

Just then, as he so deftly danced
Upon the heights, the circus chanced
Upon the place where he was sold
An age ago at three years old ...
He gambols to this day with ease
On three big bountiful banyan trees.

CYFLEITHWY

which needs a poem and a half to itself

'Yes, we've put our sleeves to sleep.'
'Yes, we've bought our links.'
'Yes, we've drunk a river of silk.'
'Yes, we've walked our stinks.'
'Yes, we've gulped our syrups down.'
'Yes, we've stopped saying Ow.'
'Yes, we've learned to be polite.'
'Yes, we're cured, and how!'

'No, we've not woken our leaves.'
'No, we've not sold our birds.'
'No, we've not eaten our boots.'
'No, we've not run out of words.'
'No, we've not upped our stakes.'
'No, we've not gone Whee!'
'No, we've not fallen ill just yet.'
'No, we can't say Cyfleithwy.'

Sez who?!

OF COURSE YOU CAN!

Cyf as in covenant
Cyf as in guv
Cyf as in coveted
Make it rhyme with love.

Leith as in sheath
Leith as in brrrr
Leith as in leeway
Leith as in grrrr.

Wy as in us
Wy as in we
Wy as in yes in French
Make it rhyme with Oui!

Measure a length of line
From your place to mine,
Got it?

Measure from yours again
On the morning train
—Keep up!—

To that one place you see
When you think of me,
Okay?

It's only then I might
(If all else is right,
Mind you),

Then calculate the way
To your side, one day ...

Move it!

PLOC
is the brick in the tumbling wall

PLOC
is the guitar strummed wrong

PLOC
is the cheese with the pizza thrown in

PLOC
is the courage of song

PLOC
is the lock to the perfect key

PLOC
is the grand tantrum of peeve

PLOC
is the flower ripped from the grass

PLOC
is waiting to leave

CULTURALLY MEANINGFUL WORDS

(One Word, Two Poems)

KATHAK

- ES

Lesson 1 is Seamlessness.
Like starlight's all-night stillness.

Lesson 2 is Listen Tight.
A style as loud as daylight.

Lesson 3: Loosen a Thread.
Unite others untethered.

Lesson 4: Write a Story.
Let one sole tell it, and see.

Lesson 5: Look Alive, Learn.
Will you spot the loose pattern?

Lesson 6: Laces in Sight.
Dare whisper the word 'respite'.

Lesson 7 is Weaving.
A humble stumble can sting.

Lesson 8 is Listeners.
Touting equals spectators.

Lesson 9: Last line lonely
And far away must end free ...

KATHAK

- SC

for Vikram Iyengar

storytelling dance
        of talking feet

mathematical dance
        with bells on

scientific dance
        with soul offbeat

poetical dance
        of neurons

CYNGHANEDD

- ES

Two unalike, two completely different people, one small, one tall,
once stepped off a train in the rain and bumped
into each other, got entangled between
a purse clasp and a coat strap,
laughed and blushed, but
not yet in love.

Two unalike, completely different people, one liked
sitting in the shade sipping strawberry juice,
one liked consuming coffee
in cold corner cafés,
not yet in love.

Two unalike, different people, like pepper
and salt, mountains and coral
reefs, definitely not
yet in love.

Two unalike, people poles apart,
at odds, clashing, not
yet in love.

Two unalike, just not
yet in love.

Two unalike, yet
in love.

CYNGHANEDD

– SC

I

Two floating swans
swimming towards a fleet of thought
shipshape as scrubbed decks
Intertwining graceful necks

II

A banner
furled a spanner
and a spoon.

A mountain
began to beguile
a beggar.

A fly
fell out of a forlorn
fountain

that gushed
golden goblets
of Fanta.

On the banks of the Hoogly River
I once saw a sliver of dye
That fluttered and muttered
From gutter to ground
And made no more sound than a sigh.

On the banks of the Hoogly River
I once saw a figure of clay,
All told it had folded
Once moulded from earth,
But none of its mirth came away.

On the banks of the Hoogly River
A curious fruit shimmered and shone,
Newfangled it dangled,
Tangled in a tree,
A neon bud daily turned on.

To the banks of the Hoogly River
In early November I'd come,
Daydreaming through seemingly
Teeming old towns
Deceivingly drowned out by drums.

'Pujo' meant nothing when I was little
growing up inside my head.

Even 'winter' meant more and 'snack-toasts'
and 'khudsides' off the mountain roads.

You have to live a word to know it.

Taste the crispy edges, bite into the
filling (cheese? tomato? mayo?).

You have to feel it scuff your knees,
see it turn your elbows green,

before you can say you know
what it really means.

And so, 'pujo' meant—nothing,
nada, zilch.

Even 'heather' meant more
because I had seen it in my dreams.

You have to dream a word to know it.
Dream its colour (purple).

Not *have* to see it to believe
it exists.

And so, 'pujo' meant nothing
high up on the hills.

Neither dreamt nor felt
neither eaten nor smelt

it stayed unknown
until

time passed.

Was I old?
Or old-er?

Or simply closer
to the word?

Close enough to watch?
Yes. And so, I watched.

I watched elders gather
on wobbly plastic chairs.

I watched youngsters hand out plates
dressed in festive wear.

I watched married women dance
with fire-bowls in their hands.

I watched the men (their husbands)
take a chance—

bite the fire-bowls between their teeth
and dance. I watched the drummers

quicken as the evening grew even longer.
As the drumbeats matched their hearts

I watched the elders become younger.
I watched the praying flowers

land on people's hair.
I watched the blue get bluer

and the lightness in the air.
I watched the face of Durga

(she was lovely).
I watched her children too

(Ganesh, Kartik, Saraswati)
and the kola-bou.

I watched the swan, the mouse,
the peacock, but most—

I watched the tiger—
lifelike enough to roar.

And I mourned all the Bengal tigers
that are no more.

I watched more than I listened
        (I shut out all unpleasant sounds—
        the too-loud microphones, the raucous
        music blasting rounds)
and suddenly I knew—

'pujo' wasn't a ritual until
you turned it into one.

It could simply be a feeling,
a letting-go of useless pride.

It could simply be going home again,
just a place to hide.

Now, when I hear the Mahalaya
and find my name being sung

(Anandomoyee—my Didima's name for me)

I remember Didima loving me
for being who I was,

never minding my hair (short), my earrings
(long), my dislike for saris (and gold).

She taught me that faith in people
was a kind of prayer (wise and bold).

I think of my own mother
who never had a pujor-ghor

and yet—

when she rang a small brass bell and blew
the conch I got her from Kanyakumari

(because I liked its mother-of-pearl hue)

when she placed a single red hibiscus
next to conch and bell—*that* was 'pujo' too.

So now, when friends
(like Eurig here, and my dear Siân)

visit my home town and are charmed
by pandals, dhakis, and the flowers,

I don't feel I'm alien as much
as I once thought I was.

And when I go with aunt and mum
and friends to the pujo in the hood,

and stand in line to eat a plate of bhog
(that yummiest of pujo-food!)

it's not because
I'm suddenly someone else, oh no!

I'm still that clueless girl who grew up
in the foothills of the Himalaya,

who didn't know then that 'pujo' was
both prayer flag and Buddhist gong,

pine cones, candles, oranges,
Christmas cake and chapel song.

Often, it takes a long, long time
for a word to make some kind of sense.

Till then, a word is empty
as is any empty, unfelt act,

like bowing your head because you're forced
to take tradition for a fact.

Believe freely, across the faiths,
in what's personal and true.

Or else forget it—
until *it* remembers and comes looking for you.

EISTEDDFOD

- ES

Three things that make a poet
Content (and don't I know it):
A crowd, a poem on a page
And one big stage to show it.

Three things that fill pavilions
With satisfied civilians:
Good poets, druids in their bling
And singers in their millions.

Three things (all things permitting)
That some see rather fitting:
A golden harp, a head of hair
And one big Chair to sit in.

EISTEDDFOD

- SC

Ever been to a mela? A bazaar? A carnival?

Have you ever wandered over fields eating ice creams
in the sun?
Ever sat down on the grass and listened to people sing?
Have you ever stood up and danced because the music
made you want to?
Ever shared a table with strangers eating picnic lunches
as they chat?
Have you ever stood in winding lines in front of vans
selling burgers and fries?
Ever seen performers and comedians speaking
into mikes?

Have you ever watched plays being staged inside cosy
little tents?
Ever entered places filled with books and come out with
your mind full of smiles?
Have you ever bought candyfloss and lollipops and
knick-knacks and sparkly tops?
Ever seen people of all ages acting like kids on
summer vacation?
Have you ever lain down on the ground so you could
feel the world turn around you?

If you have, you've already been to an Eisteddfod!

Have you ever seen people all dressed up in robes of blue
and green and white?
Ever seen a poet being crowned, and cloaked in
purple, like a king?
Have you ever seen a chair as gorgeous as the tree it's
carved from?
Ever seen a sword being sheathed in a stadium
full of people?
Have you ever heard an ancient word—PEACE!—being
pledged in voices raised as one?
Ever heard an ancient poetry being made ever-young?
Have you ever felt the air around you tingle
with mysterious joy?
Ever walked miles in wellies through muddy fields
just for fun?

Have you ever drunk water out of blue bottles
named 'dŵr'?
Ever been soaked to the skin as you waited for a friend
to meet you?
Have you ever listened to the wind blowing through
roaring seas of words?
And felt entirely at home in an unknown, enticing land?

If you haven't, it's time you went to an Eisteddfod!

CHOLO!

- ES

When all the shops
Are almost shut,
But you're in despair ...
Cholo, butt!

When poets gather,
Poems on tongues,
And the crowd is ready ...
Cholo, chums!

When your mate's behind
And needs a push,
Your bus is arriving ...
Cholo, mwsh!

When you're in the stadium
For the rugby,
And the singing's over ...
Cholo, Cymru!

CHOLO!

– SC

Cholo!
drags me out of torpor
when I’m in a mulish moment

like a secret stash of energy
that explodes
a volcano that is dormant

Cholo!
is a friendly hand
an invitation to come along

down the road
or around the bend
or five miles and a furlong

Cholo!
isn't *Hurry Up!*
unless it's said twice over

it's more like
Let's go now or else
we'll miss the landing of the rover

Neither come hither
nor comeuppance

Cholo! makes me feel less alone
because someone has to say it

it has the nicest knock-kneed ring
whichever way you play it

DA IAWN

- ES

It's what you tell a child of six
Who by some innocence still sticks
To his or her true story when
The adults shout, 'Don't lie again!'

It's what you tell a distant cloud
Who hours back in darkness vowed
To spoil your bright raincoatless day,
Before it turned and went away.

It's what you tell a friend who tries
Your awkward language on for size
And finds among old hats a crown
That fits just perfectly, 'Da iawn!'

DA IAWN

– SC

for Mererid Hopwood

If you haven't heard these words before,
You don't know what you've missed.
For these are the words you want to use
When you have just been kissed.

Or when you've won the hockey match
And brought home the silver trophy,
Or made it to the Scrabble team
By spelling 'catastrophe'!

You use them in celebration,
You use them when you're glad.
You use them in congratulation
But never ever when you're sad.

They are a gift from far away,
Each word ringing like a chime,
My friend from Wales taught them to me
And now I use them all the time!

DOSA

- ES

Wake up
Make up
With the world.

Shape up
Scrape up
Bum from bed.

Dose of
Dosa
Starts a day.

Slap it
Wrap it
Fold a feast ...

Better
Get a
Griddle greased.

Instruction manual: *foldteardipeat*
Tastebud-altering speed

BARA LAWR

- ES

From afar
It looks almost like
Caviar.

It is goo
The sea has scraped
Off its shoe.

BARA LAWR

- SC

I thought *laverbread* was simply bread
(what else could it be?)

until I got a jar of it—filled with the scent
of the sea

and black flakes that looked like coal
and—I was told—

the way to eat it was—to drop them in a bowl
of soup (called *cawl*)

So laverbread wasn't bread at all
(for sandwiches served on a plate)

but really a kind of seaweed—
what!—called *bara lawr*

which rhymes with *mawr*
which simply means *big* or *great*.

Which makes me think—if nothing is
what its name suggests—

why bother
naming things at all?

Why not call seaweed '12 o'clock'
and bread 'lamba pau'

(meaning long-legs-and-all)?
If words have gone off their

rockers, why not knock them
off their designated pegs?

Why not call a bowl of soup a 'shorba'
(which rhymes with a Greek named Zorba)?

Why not call a plate a 'thali'
or—hang on!—even 'thala'?

Why not say—instead of 'Wassup'—
simply 'Kay zhala'?

Why not call tears 'kanna'
(the Tamil word for 'dear')?

Why not call Mum 'Aai'?
(Hindi for 'Coming! I'm heeere!')

Why not call me 'mi'
(as they do in Marathi)?

Why not—instead of 'mango seed'—
say 'aamer aathi'?

And then I pause—phew!—
and recall

with relieved and loopy grin—
we can—we do—we do just that

in this polyglot world we're in!

GAMCHA

- ES

There was a guy
in Chittagong
who wore his hair
and garments long,

he was a chor-
-eographer
and quite a cool
photographer,

who through his lens
one day saw me,
and paused a while
in sympathy,

for I am used
to colder climes,
and on that day
was limp with slime

and sweat and dirt,
and lathered down
with all the heat
of that hot town,

so he came up,
and in my hand
he placed a fold
like contraband,

a red-blue swathe
of cloth run through
with strips of green
and yellow too.

'You need it, man!'
he laughed, and left,
and there I stood
as if by theft,

softly cooling,
shoaled in shade,
poet with gift
of garb arrayed,

so if the guy
in Chittagong
who wore his hair
and garments long

can hear me,
your payment's due
and that's a wrap,
this one's for you!

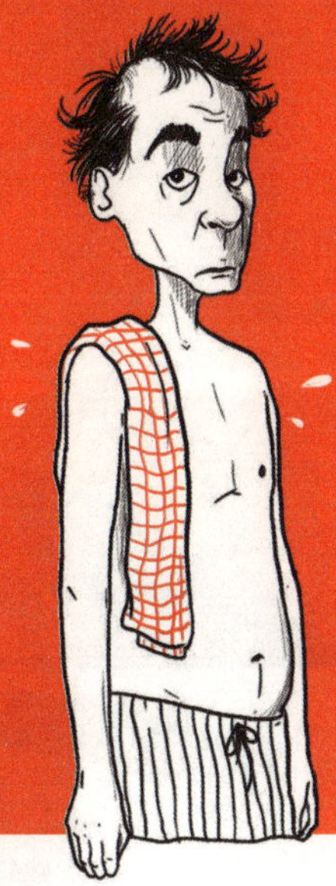

GAMCHA

– SC

A length of cloth in small red-checks-and-blue
turned artfully into swirly skirts for girls
by designers who suggest guys could wear it too,
slung casually over one shoulder or even
twisted stylish (like a scarf) in a dude-ish
'what the heck'. Originally, though,
a gamcha was merely a handy mop
for sweaty neck or brow, a thin light absorbent
towel taken to wells and bathing taps, or wrapped
around well-oiled heads or tresses (wet)
by ladies taking naps. So clearly, this is one heck
of a multipurpose piece from high-street to home
and back, traditional or radical as you like!
Now then—do *you* have one, hanging on your rack?

HIRAETH

- ES

It is the lion
You just saw.

How big
Was its paw?

Has it
Opened its jaw?

Were the sides
Of its maw

Trimmed
Jet
Black?

Its eyes
See you,

It's meal
Is due,

You know
It too.

Whatever
You do,

Don't
Look
Back!

HIRAETH

- SC

human as *insaaniyeth*
real as *asliyeth*
clear as *koifiyeth*
that old homesickness *hiraeth*

diamond-bright as tears

PLACE NAMES:

Long and Short

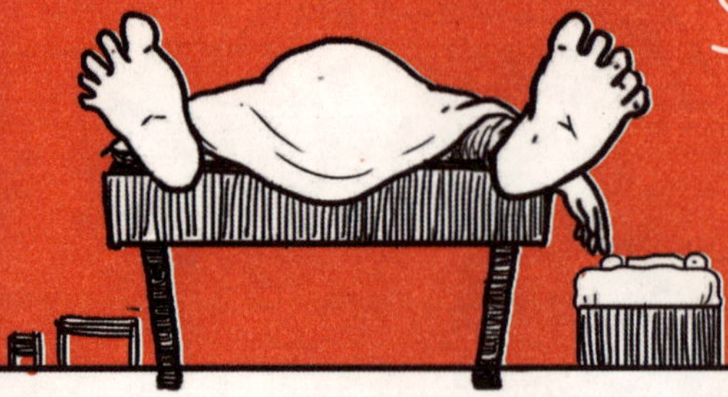

SRAVANABELAGOLA

- ES

To visit there
Is to eat like a king for six days,
But sleep on a different bed each night.

The first bed's big,
A double with silky white sheets,
But only one little measly pillow, sliver thin.

The second's huge,
A vat of sunken luxuriousness
And bounce, seven puffed pillows in a pile.

The third bed's thin
And clunky, like a digger's arm
That never fully extends, but you can order drinks.

The fourth is a flat
Savannah whose horizon cuts
Off at the edge like a sheer cliff, clean and vast.

The fifth is too
Short, toes peep out off the
Bottom, feel the darkness peer back.

The sixth bed, bare
And dogged as a hermit's,
The sleepers' slumber eased on wooden laths.

SBLOT

– SC

I think I like Sblot a lot
I might even live there forever

Never having visited (yet)
I know it'll suit me whenever
                                        I do.

You see,
Sblot reminds me of ink

And I like ink a lot
Specially when it makes a
                                        splotch!

Sblot reminds me of a place
I used to go when happy

A safe and secret
                    spot

That was never
not

Filled with the greenest
thoughts.

So,
I've decided

If I ever leave home
Sblot is where I'll go

And if you're ever
Looking for me

Sblot is where I'll be.

THIRUVANANTHAPURAM

- ES

I can smell

Pummelled dough growing into warm loaves
A sack of beans slipping over the hot lip of a cup
A single sleeve of dosa on a tava light and tough
Curled up wooden cutlets planed off the lathe

A bowl of gulab jamun in sticky syrup dipped
The crack and crunch of dusty Bombay mix
A puffed up puri deflating on greasy thumbs
The simple homely moistness of fresh rice

The faint breath of a passing satin shawl
The textured tang of just now opened books
A tarry smoking carriage waiting for the guard
The first clay cup of masala chai from the cart

LLANFAIRPWLLGWYNGYLLGOGERY-CHWYRNDROBWLLLLANTYSILIO-GOGOGOCH

- SC

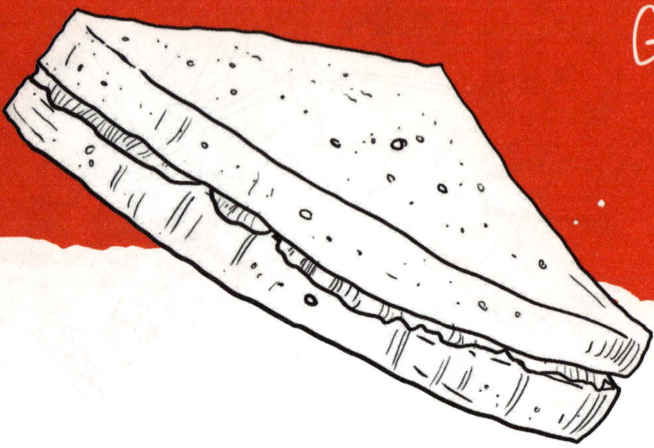

When you're feeling really angry and want to blow a fuse
Don't!
Employ a better ruse:
Breathe in and, as you slowly breathe out, say—without a single pause—
Llanfairpwllgogogoch

When you're feeling really hasty and cannot wait a milli-second
Stop!
Better than you reckoned
Is to draw yourself to fullest height and say—without a single bend—
Llanfairpwllgwyngyllgogogoch

When you're feeling really hungry and it's more than you can take
Boom!
For your growling tummy's sake
Bite down and, munching loudly, say—without a single break—
Llanfairpwllgwyngyllgogerychwyrndrobwllgogogoch

When you're feeling really pasty and don't mind letting the world know
Zoom!
Here's the way to go:
Pull out all the stops, and say—without a single pausebendbreak in flow—
Llanfairpwllgwyngyllgogerychwyrndrobwllllantysiliogogogoch

Where on earth can such a word exist?
Don't think I'm being precocious—
It's no harder to utter than
Supercalifragilisticexpialidocious!

Llanfairpwllgwyngyllgogerychwyrndrobwllllantysiliogogogoch

Where else do they find the longest words to say precisely
what they mean?
(Like 'serendipity' instead of 'chance')
Where else do they take the longest route rather than the
shortest cut?
(Like, from Sumeria to Sundance)
Where else do they spend the longest time explaining the
simplest of things?
(Like, for example, how to shut a door)
Where else do they make the longest face on hearing the
bestest news?
(Like, today my dog turned four!)

A Neat Note on 'Cynghanedd'

The second of Sampurna's two poems on page 51 includes the words

fountain, and

Fanta

Say them out loud!

Can you hear how similar they are, even though their meanings and vowel sounds are completely different?

This, in Welsh, is what we call 'cynghanedd', which means 'harmony' or 'chiming', and it's as old as the Welsh language itself (and almost all languages are pretty ancient).

But you can use 'cynghanedd' in any language, and this is how ...

Every word in every language on earth has either one or more syllables. One of those syllables always carries more weight than the others. For example, the word 'fountain' has two syllables, and the weight falls on the first syllable:

FOUNTain

It would sound really silly if the weight was on the second syllable!

fountAIN

The first syllable in this word has two vowels and three consonants:

F ou NT

In 'cynghanedd', the consonants are the most important bits, and that's because consonants are so much noisier than vowels. So we can forget about the vowels:

F—NT

Let's look now at the word 'Fanta'. The weight again falls on the first syllable:

FANTa

And the word has the same consonants as 'fountain', and in the right place:

F—NT

That's why both 'fountain' and 'Fanta' make a 'cynghanedd'. In other words, they harmonize together. The same is true of 'font', 'fantasy', 'fainted' and 'a few winters'.

Can you find any other words that harmonize together in Sampurna's poem, or in Eurig's poem on page 46?

The last line of Eurig's poem on page 50 is a full line of 'cynghanedd', and this is how it works:

Two unalike, yet in love
t n l—k / **t n l**—v

All the consonants in the first half of the line are repeated in the same order on the other side of the line. The last consonants in both halves of the line are different this time, and that's because the words 'unalike' and 'love' are stressed (unlike 'fountain' and 'Fanta', which are unstressed).

The type of 'cynghanedd' described above is the most common. Here are the other two:

A humble stumble can sting

In this 'cynghanedd', you need two words that rhyme:

humble + stumble

And the second rhyming word needs to either alliterate or make a consonantal 'cynghanedd' with the last word in the line:

STumble + STing

So: humble + stumble + sting.

The last type of 'cynghanedd' is based on rhyme alone:

This book is about cooking

The last but one syllable in the line—which must carry the weight in that word—is rhymed with another word earlier in the line:

bOOK + COOKing

It's as easy as that! Can you make any more?

A Kind of Glossary

According to Sampurna, in Bangla

- bhyabachyaka means befuddled
- mishmishey means inky-black or pitch-dark
- joborjong means odd or ungainly
- gordobh means ass
- kelenkari means disaster or scandal
- nyakami means an annoying affectation or coyness

but you can see that Eurig thinks otherwise ...

According to Eurig, in Welsh

- llamysten means sparrow-hawk
- crair means relic
- ffrwchnedd means banana

- clindarddach means rattling
- dibyn-dobyn means topsy-turvy
- dant means tooth

but Sampurna evidently thinks otherwise ...

The only time they seem to agree on the meaning of words in their respective languages is when it comes to ... *dant* which means *tooth* in Bangla AND in Welsh!

If you're wondering how to pronounce the words, check out this video we've made for you: https://www.youtube.com/watch?v=MdpuARyycsM&feature=youtu.be

Acknowledgements

A big thank you to Debjani Banerji for suggesting we write a book together for Scholastic.

To Shantanu Duttagupta, Sushmita Chatterjee, the wonderful folks at Scholastic India, and the marvellous Mukherjee twins for their art—*diolch* and *dhonnobad*!

Thanks also to Alexandra Büchler, Elin Haf Gruffydd Jones, Nicola Morgan, Sioned Puw Rowlands and Ruchira Das for enabling so many of our inter-cultural adventures.

And finally, thanks to both our families for tolerating our foibles (and feeding us well).

Meet the Authors

About the Illustrators

Saswata and Susruta Mukherjee, twin brothers from Kolkata, are illustrators and filmmakers who love creating art out of things they see around them and things they don't.